follower's journal.

A thought provoking 42-day devotional guide
designed to assist you on your journey
from fan to follower.

ARE YOU A FOLLOWER OF JESUS?

I know. I Know. You've been asked this question before. Because it's so familiar, there is a tendency to dismiss it. Not because it makes you uncomfortable. Not because it's especially convicting. The question is dismissed mostly because it doesn't feel necessary.

One of the most sobering passages of Scripture tells of a day when many who consider themselves to be followers of Jesus will be stunned to find out that He doesn't even recognize them. In the Gospel of Luke chapter 13, Jesus tells of a day where everyone who has ever lived will stand before God. On that day many who call themselves Christians and identify themselves as followers will stand confidently in front of Jesus only to hear him say, "I never knew you. Away from me." If you've just assumed you are a follower of Jesus, I pray that the video series produced by City on a Hill will either confirm that confidence or it will convict you to reevaluate your relationship with Jesus and bring you to a commitment to follow Him.

Kyle Idleman
Teaching Minister
Southeast Christian Church / Louisville, KY

ABOUT THIS LITTLE BOOK.

When fans attend a game or a theatrical production, they often receive a program. A program basically tells you what others will do – who will play quarterback, who will perform the lead. A fan then observes critiques and applauds what these others do. Though a fan may, at times, find himself living vicariously through an on-field player or on-stage actor, in actuality the fan doesn't really do anything himself.

A fan receives a program. But what does someone receive when he comes not just to observe but to get in the game, join the cast, enlist in the action? Players get play books. Actors get scripts. Soldiers get field manuals. Doers get instruction books.

And that is what this little book is intended to be, more field guide than glossy program. Admittedly, some parts of this little book are "program" describing the characters and story line portrayed in the drama. But more importantly, this little book is meant to help you discover your role on Christ's team, your storyline in God's grand production, your post among the fighting ranks.

But even above knowing your role as a follower is knowing the One you are following: to personally know your coach, your captain, your director. The best followers know intimately the one they are following.

So more than anything else, we hope this Follower's Journal will do that, help you not just follow, but know and love the One you are following.

So for the next six weeks of your Not a Fan experience, we are asking you to carry this Follower's Journal with you; to consult it each morning, noon and night for prompts, suggestions, thoughts, and encouragement. Its presence can remind you of your role as Follower rather than a mere Fan. Bring it each week to your group as well, to help you recognize and celebrate your development in the daily decision to be a **Completely**, **Committed**, **Follower** of Jesus.

week one: | fan or follower?

WEEK ONE: FAN OR FOLLOWER?
What stood out to you from Lesson 1?

_____

_____

_____

_____

DAY 1 ____/____/____

NOTE: Besides these suggestions, you can always go to the Not a Fan website for further ideas and encouragement, **www.notafan.com**.

MORNING QUOTES:
 "If anyone would come after me, he must deny himself, take up his cross daily and follow me." (Luke 9:23)

"We say to Jesus, 'I don't mind you making some changes in my life,' but Jesus wants to turn your life upside down. We say, 'I don't mind a little touch-up work' but Jesus wants complete renovation. We're thinking tune-up, He's thinking overhaul. We think a little decorating, why not, but Jesus wants a compete remodel."   – Kyle, NAF Study

MORNING SUGGESTION:

DTR: define the relationship. Take a few minutes in the space below to define your relationship with Jesus. What it is now? And what do you want it to be?

_____

_____

_____

_____

_____

_____

_____

_____

_____

NOON REMINDER:

Try taking five minutes for meditation. Close your eyes and in your mind picture Jesus. Watch Him turn, look at you and hear Him say, "If you would come after me, you must deny yourself, take up your cross, and follow me." Hear Him say these words again and again. Become aware of your reaction to His invitation. After the five minutes have passed, jot your thoughts below.

Note: Some of the suggestions, like this one, may sound a bit inane or even non-traditional. We encourage you to try each exercise with an open mind. Give it 100%. When someone takes golf lessons or martial arts training, the instructor often gives them exercises that feel awkward, uncomfortable or even irrelevant to their goal. The athlete who improves the most is usually the one who cooperates most with the training.

_____

_____

_____

_____

_____

_____

_____

_____

_____

_____

_____

EVENING REFLECTION:
Ask Jesus to reflect on your day. Say to Him, "Jesus, tell me about my day." Write whatever stands out below.

_____

_____

_____

_____

_____

_____

END OF THE DAY FOCUS:
"No one can come to me unless the Father who sent me draws him" (John 6:44)

Jesus has invited you – not just you in general, as part of the crowd, but you yourself, by name – to follow Him. Sleep with that thought of Jesus personally calling you at the forefront of your mind.

MORNING QUOTE:

"Whenever I listen to you preach, I feel like you are trying to interfere with my life." – Kyle, NAF Study

MORNING SUGGESTION:

Look ahead to what you have scheduled today. Are you willing to have Jesus interfere? Write your reply below.

_____

_____

_____

_____

_____

_____

How do you feel about your response?

_____

_____

_____

_____

_____

NOON REMINDER:

Try repeating this phrase aloud ten times, "Lord Jesus, come interfere in my life." (Again, this is one of the suggestions that may sound childish or impractical.

But what do you really have to lose in trying it?) What comes out of this little exercise for you?

_____

_____

_____

_____

_____

EVENING REFLECTION:

What did you learn today about yourself and your willingness to have Jesus interfere in your daily life? I learned…

_____

_____

_____

_____

_____

END OF DAY THOUGHT:

What would change in your spirit when it comes to Jesus interfering in your life if you believed the words, ***"For I know the plans I have for you; plans to prosper you and not to harm, plans to give you hope and a future"***? (Jeremiah 29:11) Go to sleep with these words on your lips.

MORNING QUOTE:
"Is Jesus one of many, or is He your one and only?"
– Kyle, NAF Study

MORNING SUGGESTION:
Bring a favorite worship song to mind. Place an extra chair before you. Imagine Jesus sitting in the chair.

Try singing aloud, even if softly, the words to a favorite worship song or hymn to Jesus, as he sits before you, taking it in.

After doing so, write your reaction to what you have done. Lastly, note your sense of Jesus' reaction to your worship.

_____

_____

_____

_____

_____

_____

_____

_____

NOON REMINDER:

When a person has a "one and only," he often writes love notes, even poetry, to the beloved. Before moving on with your day, write a few words to Jesus telling Him what you think of Him.

_____

_____

_____

_____

_____

_____

_____

_____

_____

_____

_____

_____

_____

_____

_____

EVENING REFLECTION:

Whatever you are doing this evening, imagine doing it with Jesus. Write one difference that makes to you.

_____

_____

_____

_____

_____

_____

_____

_____

_____

_____

_____

END OF DAY THOUGHT:

"The LORD your God is with you, He is mighty to save. He will take great delight in you, He will quiet you with His love, He will rejoice over you with singing." (Zephaniah 3:17)

You began the morning singing to Jesus. Singing to Him is fitting because He is worthy of your love since He is perfect love. As you go to sleep, imagine him singing over you - a sweet song of His commitment, protection, forgiveness and favor.

DAY 4 ___/___/___

MORNING QUOTE:

"Any of you who does not give up everything he has cannot be my disciple." (Luke 14:33)

MORNING SUGGESTION:

Who are you most tempted to put ahead of Jesus, to love more than Jesus?

_____

_____

_____

_____

_____

Try to describe why below.

_____

_____

_____

_____

What do you gain from this exercise?

_____

_____

_____

_____

NOON REMINDER:

Think again of the person you named this morning, the one who is most likely to be in competition with Jesus for preeminence in your life. For a few minutes, try holding a mental image of Jesus alongside a mental image of the person who would be in greatest competition to him. Simply become aware of what it is like when these two images are put side by side on the movie screen of your mind. As you do, compare the two below.

<u>Jesus</u> _____

_____ _____
_____ _____
_____ _____
_____ _____

What comes from this exercise?

_____

_____

_____

_____

_____

_____

EVENING REFLECTION:

Imagine saying your evening prayers to the person you are most likely to put ahead of Jesus. How would that go? How would it compare to praying to Jesus? Evaluate the difference.

_____

_____

_____

_____

_____

END OF DAY THOUGHT:

We often dream of those most important to us. Invite Jesus into your dreams.

MORNING QUOTE:

"Is your relationship with Jesus moving from casual to committed?" – Kyle, NAF Study

MORNING SUGGESTION:

Try describing the difference you see between admiration and devotion.

Admiration is...

_____

_____

_____

Devotion is...

_____

_____

_____

Which description looks most like your relationship to Jesus?

_____

_____

_____

_____

Decide which it will be for you today toward Jesus.

_____
_____
_____
_____
_____
_____
_____

NOON REMINDER:

For a few minutes, close your eyes and imagine yourself wholly devoted to Christ. Picture yourself as a totally committed follower. How would that feel? What would you do? What expression would appear on your face? What would be different? Don't rush this. Take the time to focus. After the meditation, jot your thoughts below.

_____
_____
_____
_____
_____
_____
_____
_____
_____

EVENING REFLECTION:
Close your eyes, and with Jesus, journey back through your day. As you do, confess sin as you see it, and immediately receive Jesus' forgiveness. Don't give the Evil One a foothold by holding onto your guilt.

Thank Jesus for the good things as you recall them, and imagine Him receiving your thanks. Notice anything from which you want to learn. Write your thoughts below.

_____

_____

_____

_____

_____

_____

END OF DAY THOUGHT:
Imagine Jesus praying over you like a parent would a child. What might he say?

_____

_____

_____

_____

_____

_____

DAY 6 ___/___/___

MORNING QUOTES:

"Would you please tell him that the Bible teaches moderation in all things? Would you please tell him that it doesn't have to be all or nothing?" – Kyle, NAF Study

"I know your deeds, that you are neither cold nor hot. I wish you were either one or the other! So, because you are lukewarm—neither hot nor cold—I am about to spit you out of my mouth." (Revelation 3:14-16)

MORNING SUGGESTION:

For something to be hot, it must be heated. To be cold, it must be cooled. If an object is lukewarm, then it is either being equally heated and cooled, or being neither heated nor cooled.

If you are to be hot, then you must be sufficiently heated. Every stimulus you allow in your life will either heat or cool your love for Jesus.

Today we want you to record your habits as you go through your routine. At the end of the day, we will look at which habits "heat" your passion for Jesus and which "cool" your walk with him.

The way I wake up is…

_____

_____

_____

What I do first is…

_____

_____

_____

My morning routine is…

_____

_____

_____

My food, drink, tobacco, caffeine, alcohol
and drug consumption is…

_____

_____

_____

What is most important to me in the morning is…

_____

_____

_____

The most influential thing on my mood most mornings is…

_____

_____

_____

While I drive / commute, I…

_____

_____

_____

NOON REMINDER:
Journal about your habits while at work or school.

My routine at work is…

_____

_____

_____

When I have a chance for a break I…

_____

_____

_____

Those I talk to the most are…

_____

_____

_____

The way I problem solve is…

_____

_____

_____

My food, drink, tobacco, caffeine, alcohol and drug
consumption is…

_____

_____

_____

For a pick-me-up, I…

_____

_____

_____

During my commute home, I…

_____

_____

_____

EVENING REFLECTION:
Catalogue your typical evening pattern.

When I get home, the first thing I do is…

_____

_____

_____

My exercise practice is…

_____

_____

_____

My food, drink, tobacco, caffeine, alcohol and drug consumption is…

_____

_____

_____

I spend most of the evening…

_____

_____

_____

I never miss / my favorite thing is…

_____

_____

_____

My TV habits and internet usage are …

_____

_____

_____

The way I spend my weekends is often…

_____

_____

_____

Circle the habits that warm your heart for Jesus.
Put a box around those that cool your interest in Him.

Note: we are not asking if a certain habit is sinful or
not. This question is about you and how these habits
modify your spiritual temperature.

What do you gain from this exercise?

_____

_____

_____

_____

END OF DAY THOUGHT:
Go to sleep imagining yourself "hot" tomorrow.

DAY 7 ___ / ___ / ___

MORNING QUOTES:
"From this time many of His disciples turned back and no longer followed Him." (John 6:66)

KEEP OUT - RESTRICTED AREA - AUTHORIZED PERSONNEL ONLY *"Here's another question: Are there certain areas of your life labeled 'off limits,' or does Jesus have all access?"* – Kyle, NAF Study

MORNING SUGGESTION:
Before leaving for the day, walk around your house or apartment – with Jesus beside you – asking yourself the question, is anything I am seeing off limits to Jesus? Write what you discover below.

_____

_____

_____

_____

_____

_____

NOON REMINDER:
Walk around your workplace, again with Jesus beside you. Anything you see off limits to Him? If so, write it below.

_____

_____

_____

_____

EVENING REFLECTION:
"Death. That is really what it means to follow Jesus. We choose to die to ourselves and live for Him."
– Kyle, NAF Study

Try walking around your home, saying to Jesus, "I give you this, and this, and this…" Describe below what that exercise was like for you.

_____

_____

_____

_____

_____

_____

END OF DAY THOUGHT:
Before bed, try getting on your knees and saying to Jesus, "I surrender all."

week two: **follow me**

WEEK 2: FOLLOW ME
What stood out to you from Lesson 2?

_____

_____

_____

_____

_____

_____

_____

_____

_____

_____

_____

_____

_____

_____

_____

_____

Note: As you begin your second week of using the Follower's Journal, please know that you can use this little book in any way that helps you follow. You may want to write notes and learnings beyond those asked for. Or you may want to adjust the questions or exercises to take them in a different direction you find more helpful. This is your journey so let the Holy Spirit lead you in how to use this journal.

DAY 1 __/__/__

MORNING QUOTE:

"The Bible says in Romans that all of us have sinned and fallen short of the Glory of God. In other words, none of us are good enough. We've all said things we shouldn't have said. We've all done things we shouldn't have done. And so we scrub and scrub at the stain, but the stain just won't come out.

And we reach this point, where we're not sure what to do. And so we live in denial of the stain. Or we blame other people for the stain. Or we rationalize and justify the stain. Or we just live in guilt and fear hoping somehow that no one will notice." – Kyle, NAF Study

MORNING SUGGESTION:

Be honest. What is one of your biggest stains? What failure, sin, stupidity has left a huge mark on your life? If you are willing, describe it in writing. If you are not willing, try to describe why.

_____

_____

_____

_____

_____

In the past, which of the following have you done with this stain?

__ denied it   __ ignored it   __ blamed others for it

__ rationalized it __ justified it __ lived in guilt over it

What effect have those ways of dealing with the stain had on your life?

_____

_____

_____

_____

_____

_____

_____

_____

NOON REMINDER:
As painful as it may be, take a couple of minutes to think again about some of your biggest "spills" and their subsequent stains. What images come to mind? Try drawing below what your stains might look like to Jesus. (Yes, another "silly" exercise, but try it and then notice the effect.)

EVENING REFLECTION:

As our life awareness grows, we recognize that there isn't just one stain on one couch, but all of our furniture is marred - every relationship, every effort, every day is stained in some way.

What do you do with your awareness of not just a few stains but the chronic spilling and staining in your life?

__ hide it   __fight it   __ medicate it
__ minimize it   __confess it   __ justify it

As my awareness of sin grows, I…

_____
_____
_____
_____
_____
_____

END OF DAY FOCUS:

Meditate on what sleep is like when your stains are heavy on you. Then consider what your sleep is like when you are confident your stains are removed. Decide which mindset you want to have as you sleep.

MORNING QUOTE:
"Matthew understood that to follow a Rabbi was a twenty-four hour a day commitment. Matthew understood that it was not just knowing what Jesus knows, it was going to be living how Jesus lived. Matthew understood that in order to follow Jesus, he must call Jesus Lord." – Kyle, NAF Study

MORNING SUGGESTION:
Take a few moments to imagine your morning ahead. Anticipate situations that will likely occur. In each case, picture yourself following Jesus into that situation. For example, if you wake the kids, envision yourself walking into the bedroom behind Jesus, with Him going ahead of you and showing you what to do and how to do it. Or if you have a client meeting, imagine Jesus walking into that office ahead of you, and you following His lead in how to listen, speak and act.

After taking a few minutes to picture your morning following Jesus, jot any thoughts below.

_____

_____

_____

_____

_____

_____

_____

_____

_____

NOON REMINDER:
Remember this morning's exercise?
What effect did it have on your morning?

_____

_____

_____

_____

_____

_____

_____

_____

Foresee the afternoon ahead, again picturing
Jesus going ahead of you, and you following Him.
Note below anything you want to remember.

_____

_____

_____

_____

_____

_____

_____

EVENING REFLECTION:

Review your day in your mind's eye. Notice any times
you really did mentally follow Jesus into a situation,
and allow Him to take the lead. What was it like? Also
notice the times you simply forgot or weren't willing to
let him lead. Journal what you see as the difference in
the two ways of entering situations.

_____

_____

_____

_____

_____

_____

_____

If following Jesus is indeed a twenty-four hour a day commitment, then what would it look like to follow Jesus as one rests?

_____

_____

_____

_____

_____

_____

_____

_____

_____

_____

_____

_____

_____

_____

_____

_____

_____

_____

_____

_____

_____

_____

MORNING QUOTE:

"Doulos is the Greek word for slave. A slave had no rights. A slave signed over everything to the master, even his own identity. A slave's one word job description was obey. So Matthew understood, to call Jesus Lord, was to call himself a slave." – Kyle, NAF Study

MORNING SUGGESTION:

Do you want to be radical in following Jesus? Make a list of your primary possessions – house, cars, bank accounts, etc. Then make a list of your skills – gardening, teaching, mechanical, selling, nursing, etc. Add a list of your core identities - husband, coach, leader, mother, and artist. Then sign all these over to Jesus.

Possessions	Skills	Identities

Lord Jesus, in view of your being the giver of the above, and in view of your sacrifice for me, and in view of your free gift of forgiveness and everlasting life, and in view of your great and indescribable worth, I hereby relinquish my rights over all the above to you and your will.

Signed _____

Date _____

NOON REMINDER:

As you look back on your morning, what was it like to live, or what would it have been like to have lived, those hours with all you have surrendered to Jesus?

Living surrendered to Jesus is like…

_____

_____

_____

_____

_____

_____

_____

_____

EVENING REFLECTION:
(Y / N) Did you actually sign over the possessions, skills and identities of your life to Jesus this morning? Whether you did or not, jot your reflections on what it was like even thinking about signing over all your rights to Jesus. What effect does facing a decision to actually sign on the dotted line have on you?

_____

_____

_____

_____

_____

END OF DAY REFLECTION:
What possession, skill or identity is most difficult for you to sign over to Jesus? Why?

_____

_____

_____

_____

_____

_____

Go to sleep imagining either:
1. Laying this at Jesus' feet
2. Clutching this thing to your chest while telling Jesus "no"

DAY 4 ___/___/___

MORNING QUOTE:

"I meet people every week who are slaves to something, but they found freedom when they became a slave to Jesus Christ. They were slaves to possessions or slaves to their own pleasures, they were slaves to people, what other people thought of them. But they discovered that true freedom is only found when they live as a slave to Jesus Christ. Instead of shame and bondage and death, we find joy and grace and eternal life. You will never know true freedom until you have completely surrendered and become a slave to Jesus Christ." – Kyle, NAF Study

MORNING SUGGESTION:

A fish freed from its cage called water is a pitiful sight, struggling, reeling, and gasping for breath. For a fish, to be freed from the constraints called water is to be enslaved in a foreign world. Think of a particularly tempting sin. When you throw yourself into that sin, what results?

To what does that life inevitably lead to?

_____

_____

_____

_____

_____

_____

_____

_____

Determine whether or not living in that sin is indeed like being a fish out of water.

NOON REMINDER:
Try saying the following out loud and noticing how you feel when you say each:

- I will be a slave to pleasure.
- I will be a slave to possessions.
- I will be a slave to what other people think.
- I will be a slave to money.
- I will be a slave to sex.
- I will be a slave to status.
- I will be a slave to my career.
- I will be a slave to my family.
- I will be a slave to Jesus.

What is your reaction to this exercise?

_____

_____

_____

_____

_____

_____

EVENING REFLECTION:
To what do you tend to become enslaved? Money? People's opinions? Yourself? Try this exercise (actually doing it will be much more powerful than merely thinking about it).

First, create an altar to whatever you are most likely to become enslaved. For example, if you tend to be enslaved to alcohol, make an altar to it by setting a six pack or wine bottle on a chair or low table. If it is sex, maybe set the laptop on which you view pornography on the chair. If it is a certain person's opinion, you might put their picture on the altar.

If it is yourself, you might place a mirror on the altar. Then kneel before the "altar" as if in worship.

Really try it. How does it feel? What comes to mind?

What is it like to give yourself to this thing?
Write your feelings and thoughts.

_____

_____

_____

_____

Try to remember this image the next time you are
excited by the prospect of giving yourself to this idol.

END OF DAY FOCUS:
Before bed, you might set up an altar to Jesus beside
your bed, using whatever memento most dearly
represents Him to you. Kneel there and place your
allegiance with him. How does that feel?

_____

_____

_____

_____

_____

_____

_____

_____

_____

DAY 5 ____/____/____

MORNING QUOTE:
"She wants a divorce."
– Kyle, NAF Study

MORNING SUGGESTION:
Like Eric in our drama, we've all had to say things we never thought we would have to say, such as: she wants a divorce, I am addicted, I am sorry I hit you, I had an abortion, I was fired, you are not my first lover, and so on. Think of the hardest things you have had to say because you hadn't been following Jesus. They will be painful to write, but the pain of recall can protect you from the pain of repeat.

_____

_____

_____

_____

_____

What don't you want to have to say at the end of this day?

_____

_____

_____

_____

NOON REMINDER:
Meditate on the following words.
Circle those that stand out to you today.

"If being a slave to sin has left you broken and bruised and you find your life is in pieces...

...my master loves you and if you let him, He'll take the pieces of your life and turn them into a beautiful mosaic. My master invites all who are weary and heavy burdened to come to him and find rest for your souls because his yoke is easy and his burden is light. And when you became a slave to my master, He makes you His son."

EVENING REFLECTION:
If Christ makes a mosaic from our sin, what has he done with yours? Look over the difficult sentences you listed this morning. How could each be rewritten because of what Jesus has done for you?

For example, "She wants a divorce" could become, "I saw I was a jerk and learned to love her again" or "My divorce broke me open and though we didn't get back together I know now I have to lean on Jesus in everything I do."

END OF DAY FOCUS:
What sentence do you want on your lips as you go to bed tonight?

_____

_____

_____

_____

_____

_____

_____

_____

_____

_____

_____

_____

_____

MORNING QUOTE:

"When Jesus said to Matthew, 'Follow me,' He was making it clear His invitation to follow is not just for the religious elite, for the morally upright or for those who have their lives together. His invitation is for all of us who are hiding stains.

Jesus said, 'Anyone who would come after me, must deny himself, take up his cross daily and follow me.' (Luke 9:23) 'Anyone' is a pretty inclusive word. Anyone can follow Jesus. Anyone who ever thought to themselves, 'I've gone too far...my stains are too big...'. Anyone who has ever lain awake at night and said 'I can't believe what I have done'. Anyone who has ever looked in the mirror and said to themselves, 'I can't believe what I have become.' Anyone can follow.

Anyone who knows down deep that they've got really nothing to offer Jesus. Really, it's what Jesus offers us that changes things. On the day He said to Matthew, 'Follow me,' something changed in him that day. And how do we know all this about Matthew's life? How do we know about his past failures and mistakes? Because he tells us."
– Kyle, NAF Study

MORNING SUGGESTION:
Read the morning quote out loud,
while standing in front of a mirror.

Note your reaction.

_____

_____

_____

_____

_____

_____

_____

NOON REMINDER:
Read today's morning quote again, slowly. Write below
what you think Jesus is saying to you through it.

_____

_____

_____

_____

_____

_____

_____

EVENING REFLECTION:

Anyone who looks at themselves honestly knows they have nothing to offer God. It's what God offers us that changes things.

Complete this sentence as if Jesus were speaking to you:

" _____ (your name), I am offering you…

Write your response.

_____

_____

_____

_____

_____

_____

_____

_____

_____

_____

END OF DAY FOCUS:

Tell Jesus your response to his invitation again before you close your eyes in sleep.

DAY 7 ____/____/____

MORNING QUOTE:

*"Morgan, you could never make a stain
so big that it would keep us from loving you."*
– Kyle, NAF Study

MORNING SUGGESTION:

Try substituting your name in the sentence above. Say it aloud. Now imagine hearing Jesus say those words to you. Hear Him say it several times. Become aware of your inner response to these words. Write your response below.

_____

_____

_____

_____

_____

_____

Is that the mindset in which you want to live out this day? Why?

_____

_____

_____

_____

NOON REMINDER:

Sit and close your eyes, and hear again Jesus speak the words, "You could never make a stain big enough to keep me from loving you." Imagine yourself fully accepting these words, agreeing with them, believing them. If you did, what effect would it have on your…

- emotions
- closest relationships
- outlook on life
- feeling toward Jesus

EVENING REFLECTION:

"When Morgan trusted her parents' unconditional love was real, she not only admitted her stain, she bragged about it. Her stain came to represent her total acceptance." – Kyle, NAF Study

Imagine absorbing the words, "_____, you could never make a stain big enough to keep me from loving you." Imagine those words soaking into the very fabric of your being the way the finger nail polish soaked into the white couch. Imagine these words becoming a "stain" on your soul that won't come out – in this case, a good stain, a permanent mark that the world can never scrub away.

You may want to add to your meditation with an experience such as:

- Laying in a warm bath surrounded by candles, visualizing the water as the unconditional love of Jesus covering you.
- Sitting in a hot shower experiencing the constant stream of water as Jesus repeatedly reassures you that nothing can separate you from his love.
- Turning up your favorite instrumental music and sensing the melody surrounding you as the embodiment of the words, "You can never make a stain big enough to keep me from loving you."
- Sitting in your favorite outdoor spot re-interpreting the enveloping splendor as a visual reminder of Christ's never ending love.

END OF THE DAY FOCUS:
Let your mattress, sheets and blankets be the words, "_____, you can never make a stain big enough to keep Jesus from loving you. "

week three: **what must I do?**

WEEK 3: WHAT MUST I DO?

Write your responses to the final questions of the group session here.

What, if anything, do you think Jesus is asking you to give up these days?

_____
_____
_____
_____
_____

How do you determine that He is asking this of you?

_____
_____
_____
_____
_____

What do you see yourself doing about it?

_____
_____
_____
_____
_____

MORNING QUOTE:
*"On this trail called life, all of us are following
someone's directions. None of us are really blazing
our own trail. We all follow a path that's been laid
out for us by someone claiming to know the way.
The question is: whose directions are you following?
What path are you on?"* – Kyle, NAF Study

MORNING SUGGESTION:
Try this, even though it might sound childish.

Draw a winding path, and on it a stick figure that
represents you. Then draw a large sign post. On the
sign, name the path you are on. It might be called
"Dad's Trail" if you have basically been following in
your father's footsteps. Or it might be "Easy Lane"
in view of the fact that you do whatever seems easiest.
It could be "Wall Street" because for you it has been
all about the money. Or it might be "Service Street"
as you are truly striving to put others first. In any case,
be honest. Name the road you are on.

Try to describe in three sentences or less why you have chosen this path.

_____
_____
_____
_____
_____
_____
_____
_____

NOON REMINDER:

Look back over your morning, and the way you lived it. Whose path was it that you followed? Workaholic Drive? Avoidance Alley? Lover's Lane? How do you feel about the path of your morning?

_____
_____
_____
_____
_____
_____
_____
_____

Every moment is a fork in the road. You can stay on the current path or turn to a new way. Would it be a good idea to stay on your morning road or take a new way? If take a new way, what would it be named?

_____

_____

_____

_____

_____

EVENING REFLECTION:
If you stay with the path you are currently on, where will it lead in 10 years? Draw the path again, but leave room to describe its destination.

_____

_____

_____

_____

_____

END OF DAY FOCUS:
Picture the destination of the path you are on as vividly as you can. Can you rest peacefully knowing that is where you are headed? If not, picture the place you want to end up. Go to sleep with that destination in mind.

MORNING QUOTE:
"Ultimately, what separates a fan from a follower is commitment. Many consider themselves followers, but what happens when their commitment is tested?"
– Kyle, NAF Study

MORNING SUGGESTION:
Ask the Holy Spirit to bring to mind a time recently when your commitment was tested - and you passed the test! Describe what happened below.

_____
_____
_____
_____
_____
_____

How did it feel recalling and describing a victory like that?

_____
_____
_____
_____
_____
_____

What do you learn from this exercise of recalling victory?

_____

_____

_____

_____

_____

NOON REMINDER:

Were you tested this morning? Almost certainly you were, if even in a small way. Describe the test, however minor or significant, and what you learned from it.

_____

_____

_____

_____

_____

_____

How does writing about this test affect you?

_____

_____

_____

_____

_____

_____

EVENING REFLECTION:
Think of someone whose commitment to
Jesus you admire.

If you were to write a personal note thanking them
for their inspiration and dedication, what would it
say? Jot a sample below. After completing it, decide
whether or not you might actually send it.

_____

_____

_____

_____

_____

_____

_____

_____

_____

_____

_____

_____

_____

END OF DAY FOCUS:
Go to sleep with this person you admire on your mind.

DAY 3 ___/___/___

MORNING QUOTE:

"Fans want to follow Jesus, but not in a way that interferes with their lives. According to some recent research I came across, sixty-five percent of American adults between the ages of eighteen and forty-two, would agree with this statement: 'I have made a personal commitment to Jesus that is still important.'

Now on the surface, that seems pretty good. Sixty-five percent is impressive, but according to that same research, these committed Christians lived a life-style that was quote 'Statistically equivalent to that of non-Christians.' So when asked about their activities from the previous thirty days, Christians were just as likely as non-Christians to have gambled, to have visited a pornographic website, to have taken something that didn't belong to them.

They were just as likely to have gotten drunk and been involved with physical abuse. They were just as likely to have lied and talked badly behind someone's back. See, they said they were committed, but they weren't completely committed. Fans try to compartmentalize their life." – Kyle, NAF Study

MORNING REFLECTION:

Circle your honest viewpoint.

Getting high is…	ok	not ok	it depends
Sex outside of marriage is…	ok	not ok	it depends
Lying to protect myself is…	ok	not ok	it depends
Getting back at someone I don't like is…	ok	not ok	it depends
Viewing porn occasionally is…	ok	not ok	it depends
Stealing from a greedy corporation is…	ok	not ok	it depends
Leaving my marriage if I'm unhappy is…	ok	not ok	it depends
Doing whatever feels good is…	ok	not ok	it depends

Would Jesus agree with your responses?

_____

_____

_____

_____

NOON REMINDER:

When we do our own thing in spite of what Jesus has said about it, then we are acting like we know better than Jesus. Choose one area where you disagree with Jesus and try completing this sentence.

I know better than Jesus when it comes to

_____ (area of disagreement)

and the reasons I believe I know better are…

_____

_____

_____

_____

_____

_____

_____

What do you see from this exercise?

_____

_____

_____

_____

_____

_____

_____

_____

EVENING REFLECTION:

Think of a time in the past when you disagreed with Jesus over how to live your life, and you did it your way. Recount what you decided, why, and how it turned out.

What I decided:

_____

_____

_____

_____

Why:

_____

_____

_____

_____

_____

How it turned out:

_____

_____

_____

_____

_____

What does answering these questions show you?

_____

_____

_____

_____

_____

_____

_____

_____

_____

_____

END OF DAY FOCUS:
This is what the LORD says—your Redeemer, the Holy One of Israel: *"I am the LORD your God, who teaches you what is best for you, who directs you in the way you should go. If only you had paid attention to my commands, your peace would have been like a river, your righteousness like the waves of the sea."* (Isaiah 48:17-18)

Which phrase stands out to you from this section of Scripture? Go to sleep repeating that phrase over and over in your mind.

MORNING QUOTE:

"Jesus made it clear. There is no such thing as 'selective allegiance.' When we decide to follow Him, He calls for a complete commitment and total surrender." – Kyle, NAF Study

Picture Jesus in your mind standing before you, and saying to you, "Will you follow me today?"

Write your response below.

_____

_____

_____

_____

_____

_____

_____

_____

_____

_____

_____

_____

_____

_____

NOON REMINDER:

This may sound like another crazy idea - but why not try it? Place a chair near you. Imagine Jesus sitting in it. Talk to Jesus about your day so far – your concerns, decisions, and hopes. If you are concerned others might see you talking to an empty chair, you might try holding a phone up to your ear or putting in your ear bud so they can conclude you are just on the phone (and, in a way, you are "on the phone").

EVENING REFLECTION:

Whose advice are you most likely to follow in each area?

	PERSON'S NAME	JESUS
RELATIONSHIPS		
MONEY		
SEX		
CAREER		
PARENTING		

If it isn't Jesus, compare each source to Him.
Why would you follow one over the other?

_____
_____
_____
_____
_____
_____
_____
_____
_____
_____

END OF DAY FOCUS:
If you could have someone orchestrate your dreams
while you sleep, who would it be?

_____
_____
_____
_____
_____
_____
_____

DAY 5 ____/____/____

MORNING QUOTE:

C. S. Lewis in his book, *Mere Christianity*, summarizes the call of Jesus this way: *"Give me all. I don't want so much of your time and so much of your money and so much of your work: I want you…No half-measures are any good. I don't want to cut off a branch here and a branch there. I want to have the whole tree down. I don't want to drill the tooth, or crown it, or stop it, but to have it out. Hand over the whole natural self, all the desires which you think are innocent, as well as the ones you think are wicked-the whole outfit."*

Journal your reaction to today's quote.

_____

_____

_____

_____

_____

_____

_____

_____

_____

_____

NOON REMINDER:
Imagine giving over the next five minutes to
Jesus, and keeping the rest of the day to yourself.

Next, imagine giving the whole rest of the day to Jesus.

Which option will you choose, and why?

_____
_____
_____
_____
_____
_____
_____
_____

EVENING REFLECTION:
Describe your favorite part of this day.

_____
_____
_____
_____
_____
_____
_____
_____

Describe your least favorite part of the day.

_____

_____

_____

_____

_____

_____

_____

What do you learn from answering these two questions?

_____

_____

_____

_____

_____

_____

_____

_____

END OF DAY FOCUS:
Read the morning quote three more
times. Go to sleep focusing on
whatever thought is strongest.

MORNING QUOTE:
"Fans want to follow Jesus closely enough to get all the benefits, but not so close that he calls them to sacrifice or surrender things that are important."
– Kyle, NAF Study

"If you're unsure if you're a fan or a follower, then ask yourself this: 'When was the last time my relationship with Jesus cost me something?'"
– Kyle, NAF Study

MORNING REFLECTION:
Answer Kyle's question - when was the last time your relationship with Jesus cost you something?

_____

_____

_____

_____

How do you feel about the cost?

_____

_____

_____

_____

NOON REMINDER:

Did following Jesus cost you anything this morning, if only a little discomfort in not gossiping when you felt an urge to or listening to a needy co-worker when you didn't feel like it? Describe the cost below.

EVENING REFLECTION:

"Flexitarian is a good way to describe how many people today view their commitments. They are committed...until it gets inconvenient." Were you a flexitarian today? If so, describe one of your "forbidden meats."

How did you feel after eating this meat?

END OF DAY FOCUS:

Everything cost something. Even the "easy way," the way of low commitment, has its price. Sleep all day and it will cost you your physical vitality. Procrastinate on a work project and it costs you frustration and anxiety later. The real question is: what do you end up getting for the cost you paid? Think of something you know Jesus is asking you to do that will cost you, but instead of focusing on the cost, go to sleep focusing on the end result, the final reward.

DAY 7 _____/_____/_____

MORNING QUOTE:

"Sell your possessions and give to the poor, and you will have treasure in heaven. Then come follow me."
(Matthew 19:21)

"Do you see what Jesus does here? He says to the man here is the path you're on. Here are the directions you're following. But you can't follow two sets of directions, so sell your stuff and come follow me. At some point or another, in one way or another, all of us will have such a test of commitment where our devotion will be determined and our allegiance will be exposed. Jesus will not share you. He won't share you any more than a wife will share her husband or a husband, his wife. He wants all of you." – Kyle, NAF Study

MORNING SUGGESTION:

Can you picture Jesus as jealous, wanting you but not wanting to share you with other "gods"? Put your name in the blank below, then close your eyes and hear Jesus saying these very words to you.

"_____, I want you. I am jealous for you. You are important to me. I don't want to see you used and hurt by others. I will not share you with the gods of this world."

If you really can hear these words from Jesus, what emotion, what reaction, do they elicit?

Write your response.

_____

_____

_____

_____

_____

_____

_____

NOON REMINDER:

The problem with this man is not that he had lots of money. The problem is that money had him. What has "had" you so far today? Describe whoever or whatever has "had" you in the space below.

_____

_____

_____

_____

_____

_____

EVENING REFLECTION:

Circle what stands out to you from the paragraphs below:

"Some of you know you can't find satisfaction in a box. You can't buy happiness off a rack or order it off the internet or drive it off a lot." – Kyle, NAF Study

"They exchanged their Glory for an image of a bull, which eats grass" (Psalm 106:20). That's just not a good trade. Have you exchanged the glory of God for a car that can really handle the corners? Have you exchanged the glory of God for a job that He hasn't called you to, but pays really well? Have you exchanged the glory of God for a house that has all the upgrades? These things are all fine and good, but we have turned good things into God things. Fans of Jesus hold back because they're afraid they will miss out. Followers of Jesus go all in and find that when they finally let go, they discover what they really wanted all along.

"I wonder what happened to the rich young ruler. He walked away sad, but that's all we know. I wonder if he went on to become a richer older ruler." – Kyle, NAF Study

"We have left everything to follow you! What then will we get?" Jesus answered, "No one who has left home or brothers or sisters or mother or father or children or fields for me and the gospel will fail to receive a hundred times as much in this present age and in the age to come and will inherit eternal life."
(Mark 10:28-30)

"No matter what following Jesus costs us in this life, in the end we won't see it as a sacrifice. Rather we will see it as a privilege and an honor." – Kyle, NAF Study

END OF DAY FOCUS:
Enter sleep thinking of one phrase from the paragraphs you just read. Imagine it coming alive, taking on a life of its own, teaching you.

week four: **bury the dead!**

WEEK 4: BURY THE DEAD
What stood out to you from Lesson 4?

_____

_____

_____

_____

_____

_____

_____

_____

_____

DAY 1 ___/___/___

MORNING QUOTE:
"Sometimes in an effort to get as many people as possible to follow Jesus I have, with good intentions, made following Him sound as attractive and appealing as possible...I realized that I have been guilty of selling Jesus. And in emphasizing only the parts about Jesus that I thought people would like, and begging people to follow Him, I have unintentionally belittled Him...I'm sorry if I've ever cheapened Jesus or made it sound like we're doing Him a favor by choosing to follow."
– Kyle, NAF Study

MORNING SUGGESTION:
Why do you follow Jesus?

List the reasons that come to mind first.

1. _____

2. _____

3. _____

4. _____

5. _____

Do you find your reasons for following Jesus have more to do with…

[ ] what Jesus offers you – forgiveness,
      answered prayer, eternal life, etc.

[ ] what He is like – His flawless integrity,
      His bottomless love, His selfless sacrifice, etc.

NOON REMINDER:
Take a few minutes to describe why Jesus is
worthy to be followed.

Jesus, you are worthy for me to follow because…

EVENING REFLECTION:
"If you were interested in getting to know my daughter,
you had better come with everything you got; or I'll send
you packing." Do you find yourself interested in knowing
Jesus – not only what He commands and not just His
will for your life – but He Himself, His very personhood?

Yes, definitely! / Not sure, maybe? / No, not really.

Try to describe why you are passionately seeking to know Him, dispassionately seeking to know Him or not seeking to know Him at all.

_____

_____

_____

_____

_____

_____

_____

END OF DAY FOCUS:

Bring to mind your mental picture of Jesus, how you see Him in your mind when you think of Him. Don't rush ahead to the words below. First realize how you see or sense Jesus when you think of Him.

Does this mental picture contain or portray the qualities you described today at noon? For example, if you said Jesus is full of love, is your mental representation of Jesus bursting with love? If not, add depth and color and weight to your mental picture of Jesus so that it aligns with your description. That is, make your mental image match what you believe that Jesus is really like. Go to sleep meditating on this more accurate mental representation of Jesus.

MORNING QUOTE:

"This man says to Jesus, **'I will follow you wherever you go.'** (Luke 9:57) *Jesus says,* **'Foxes have holes and birds of the air have nests, but the Son of Man has no place to lay his head.'"** (Luke 9:58)   – Kyle, NAF Study

MORNING SUGGESTION:

Weigh this question in your mind. Would you rather be homeless with Jesus or have a beautiful home without Jesus? Journal your thoughts.

_____

_____

_____

_____

_____

_____

_____

_____

NOON REMINDER:

Focus on your mental image of Jesus from last night. Meditate on His glory, beauty, kindness. Imagine Him coming to you and saying, "I see you. I know you. I love you. I will never leave you."

After meditating in this way, see if you can honestly hum or sing the words to this old hymn:

I'd rather have Jesus than silver or gold;

I'd rather be His than have riches untold;

I'd rather have Jesus than houses or lands;

I'd rather be led by His nail-pierced hand

Than to be the king of a vast domain,

Or be held in sin's dread sway;

I'd rather have Jesus than anything

This world affords today.

I'd rather have Jesus than men's applause;

I'd rather be faithful to His dear cause;

I'd rather have Jesus than worldwide fame;

I'd rather be true to His holy name

EVENING REFLECTION:
As you look back on your day, what did you want?

_____

_____

_____

_____

_____

What did you get today?

_____

_____

_____

_____

_____

_____

_____

What do you think of what you wanted and
what you got?

_____

_____

_____

_____

_____

_____

_____

END OF DAY FOCUS:
Bring to mind your improved mental picture of
Jesus. Make up your own words to the song,
I'd Rather Have Jesus. You would rather have Jesus
than what? Enter sleep constructing and humming
those personal words to Him.

DAY 3 ___/___/___

MORNING QUOTE:
*"Please make trails wider
so we can hold hands while hiking."*

"Please avoid building trails that go uphill."

*"Please spray the area to get rid
of the bugs and the spiders."*

*"A small deer broke into our camp and ate
much of our food. Could we please be reimbursed?"*

– Complaints registered at the Bridger Wilderness Area

Even though some of them might sound silly, what are
your honest complaints about what it is like to follow
Jesus?

_____

_____

_____

_____

_____

_____

_____

"And I don't care how you position it, carrying a cross just isn't comfortable." – Kyle, NAF Study

Following Christ does not mean denying that the journey is hard. Can you accept that your Christian walk will often be narrow, uphill, rocky and sometimes dangerous? Journal your thoughts.

_____

_____

_____

_____

_____

_____

_____

_____

_____

_____

NOON REMINDER:
Bring to mind your mental impression of Jesus. If not already present, add to the image nail scars.

What effect does that addition have on your heart?

EVENING REFLECTION:
Bring to Jesus in prayer the complaints that you listed this morning regarding how hard it is to follow Him.

What kind of response to your complaints do you think you receive from him? Describe it below.

_____

_____

_____

_____

_____

_____

_____

_____

_____

END OF DAY FOCUS:
Bring to mind your mental image of Jesus again. If your image is not already filled with compassion, fill your representation of Jesus with compassion, as much compassion as there is in the universe. Then imagine bringing your complaints, along with your grief and troubles of the day, to Him.

What is it like?

_____

_____

_____

_____

_____

MORNING QUOTE:

"Jesus has many who love the kingdom of God, but few who bear a cross. He has many who desire His comfort, but few who desire His suffering. All want to rejoice with him, but few are willing to suffer for Him. He writes; there are many who admire his miracles, but there are few who follow in the humiliation of the cross." – Thomas à Kempis

Which words below best describes your internal reaction to today's reading? Or, if you prefer, add your own words.

shame	excitement	guilt	frustration
anxiety	joy	determination	fear
hope	pride	boredom	

Try to describe why these words are your reaction to the reading.

_____

_____

_____

_____

_____

NOON REMINDER:

What has been your primary emotion this morning?

shame	excitement	guilt	frustration
anxiety	joy	determination	fear
hope	pride	boredom	

Try to describe why.

_____

_____

_____

_____

_____

_____

_____

_____

_____

EVENING REFLECTION:

One more time, describe your primary emotion, this time what it has been since noon.

shame	excitement	guilt	frustration
anxiety	joy	determination	fear
hope	pride	boredom	

Try once more to describe why.

_____

_____

_____

_____

_____

_____

Would Jesus want this to be your primary emotion in
regard to His high call?

_____

_____

_____

_____

_____

_____

What would He want it to be?

_____

_____

_____

_____

_____

_____

_____

END OF DAY FOCUS:

Dwell on the emotion you believe Jesus primarily
wants in you when it comes to His call on your life.

Imagine yourself filled with this emotion
as you go to sleep.

MORNING QUOTE:
*"Jesus says to him, **'Follow me.'** but the man replied,
'Lord, first let me go and bury my father.' Jesus said
to Him, **'Let the dead bury their own dead, but you go
and proclaim the kingdom of God.'"***   (Luke 9: 59-60)

MORNING SUGGESTION:
Complete your own answer.
Lord, I will follow you, but first let me…

_____

_____

_____

_____

_____

_____

_____

_____

NOON REMINDER:
*"We treat our relationship with Jesus like the
diet we keep meaning to start. I'm going to start
eating right…as soon as I finish off this chicken
chimichanga."*   – Kyle, NAF Study

This seems like an appropriate quote for lunchtime!

What are you putting off that Jesus is asking you
to do today?

_____

_____

_____

_____

_____

_____

What does putting this off do **FOR** you?

_____

_____

_____

_____

_____

_____

What does putting this off do **TO** you?

_____

_____

_____

_____

_____

_____

_____

EVENING REFLECTION:
Kyle mentioned the "As now, so then principle."
What I am today, unless I take decisive action, will
be as I will be tomorrow. If as you are now, you will
always be, what will you be for the rest of your life?

_____

_____

_____

_____

_____

_____

_____

_____

What do you think of this description?

_____

_____

_____

_____

_____

_____

_____

_____

END OF DAY FOCUS:
Imagine yourself as you hope to be someday.

DAY 6 ___/___/___

MORNING QUOTE:

"Jesus calls us to take up a cross and die. Not some-day when we take our last physical breath, but to die to ourselves today...Bruce Thielemann is an author, he wrote these words, 'Please don't say anything to me about tomorrow. Tomorrow is a word the Bible does not know. The Holy Spirit's word is "today."' The Bible says, 'Today, if you hear his voice, do not harden your hearts' (Hebrews 3:15). *Today is the day of salvation. Don't say tomorrow. The word is 'today.'"*
– Kyle, NAF Study

What will you do – what will you be – today?
Portray it in words below.

NOON REMINDER:
It is still today. What do you find yourself putting off for tomorrow that you are being called to today?

_____

_____

_____

_____

EVENING REFLECTION:
What do you wish you had done, or been
or said today? I wish I had…

_____

_____

_____

_____

_____

_____

_____

END OF DAY FOCUS:
Today is over, never to return. But God is not stuck in today. "His compassions never fail. They are new every morning" (Lamentations 3:22-23). Go to sleep looking forward to meeting Jesus' compassion in the morning.

DAY 7 ___/___/___

MORNING QUOTE:

'I will follow you, Lord; but first let me go back and say good-by to my family'...But Jesus says to him, 'No one who puts his hand to the plow and looks back is fit for service in the kingdom of God.'"
(Luke 9:61-62)

What is your "but first"? I will follow but first let me... have some fun, build this house, get married, make a million dollars? Whatever your "but first" is, imagine enjoying, accomplishing or gaining that. Describe what that would be like.

_____

_____

_____

_____

_____

_____

_____

_____

_____

_____

_____

_____

At that time, will you really be any more likely to fully follow Jesus? Will you be less likely?

_____

_____

_____

_____

_____

_____

NOON REMINDER:

Bride: "Can we skip over the 'for richer or for poorer' section; I'm not ready to sign up for that."
Groom: "And can we cut the 'forsaking all others' bit? I don't want to tie myself down. I want to keep my options open."

What have you found yourself tempted to say to Jesus today?

Lord can we just skip…

_____

_____

_____

_____

_____

And Jesus can we just cut out the…

_____

_____

_____

_____

What does He reply?

_____

_____

_____

_____

EVENING REFLECTION:

"When we try to follow Jesus without dying, we find ourselves frustrated with our failure and tired of trying. Following Jesus doesn't mean that you keep trying, it means that you keep dying." – Kyle, NAF Study

How would you portray this last week for you, as "trying" or "dying"?

_____

_____

_____ __

_____

_____

Which would be easier- trying or dying?

_____

_____

_____

_____

_____

_____

_____

_____

Which do you really want to do?

_____

_____

_____

_____

_____

_____

_____

_____

END OF DAY FOCUS:
Imagine your negative self, your old self, your
selfish self, dying as you sleep; and a new self
awaking, a Christ-filled, hope-saturated, love-
centered person resurrecting with the new day.

week five: dead men's bones

AFTER GOD'S O

not a fan.

WEEK 5: DEAD MEN'S BONES

What stood out to you from Lesson 5?

_____

_____

_____

_____

_____

_____

DAY 1 ___ / ___ / ___

MORNING QUOTE:

"Those people are where they are for a reason. You work hard, you live a good life, and you get ahead. There are rules in life. All the good intentions in the world can't change that." – Bill, NAF Study

MORNING SUGGESTION:

In the video, these words tumble out of Bill's mouth naturally. His words are what might be called Bill's worldview. It is how he sees life. It is how he believes the world works. A worldview is what automatically comes to mind when we are proving our point, defending ourselves, explaining things to our kids, and so on. In our minds, this is just the way it really is.

Complete the sentences below with your automatic thoughts – not what you wished you thought, but how you really see life.

People are... _____

The way to get ahead is... _____

The most important thing in life is... _____

I am... _____

When you mess up... _____

The way to be happy is... _____

God is... _____

NOON REMINDER:
How did you live your morning?
What rules were most important?

_____
_____
_____
_____
_____

EVENING REFLECTION:

Try to put your true worldview in words again.

The purpose of life is… _____

The most important thing in life is… _____

What makes me who I am is… _____

Everyone ought to… _____

Jesus is… _____

When it comes to your worldview, with what would Jesus agree?

_____

_____

_____

_____

With what would He disagree?

_____

_____

_____

_____

END OF DAY FOCUS:

Go to sleep with the question in mind: Could I be wrong about some things I have long thought were totally true?

DAY 2 ___/___/___

MORNING QUOTE:

"Fans are very much caught up in an outward appearance. They think that somehow God is going to be impressed with their religious rule keeping or rituals or their traditions. There's nothing wrong with those things, in and of themselves. The problem comes when we do those things and it's not out of a pursuit of Jesus or a relationship with Him, but as a way to prove or measure our own spirituality." – Kyle, NAF Study

MORNING REFLECTION:

What are the primary "Christian" things you do? Prayer? Worship attendance? Morning quiet time? Working this journal? Going to small group? List the "Christian" things you do in the left hand column.

In the right hand column, list your primary motivation or reason for doing what you wrote on the left side. Are you doing it because you should? To be a good example to others? To avoid guilt? To become a better person? Because others expect it? Because you always have? To know Jesus better? To avoid Hell?

"Christian" Things I Do	My Motivation

What do you learn from your answers?

_____

_____

_____

_____

_____

_____

_____

_____

_____

_____

NOON REMINDER:

Why are you doing this "noon reminder"?
So you can feel good that you completed each
page? So you can tell the group you did it?
To ward off temptation? To reconnect to Jesus?

_____

_____

_____

_____

_____

_____

_____

Whatever your reason, imagine you are now spending
this brief time because Jesus is so cool, so worthy, so
loving, so desirous, that you just want to be filled with
His presence all the more.

What would having such an attitude be like for you?

_____

_____

_____

_____

_____

_____

_____

EVENING REFLECTION:
If you really wanted to know Jesus, to be filled with Him, to experience Him, to fully see Him, what kinds of things would you do to make that happen?
Journal your thoughts.

_____

_____

_____

_____

_____

_____

_____

_____

END OF DAY FOCUS:
Which of the things you listed above could you do while awaiting sleep?

_____

_____

_____

_____

_____

_____

_____

_____

DAY 3 ___/___/___

MORNING QUOTE:

"It doesn't matter how accurate you are if you are aiming at the wrong goal." – Kyle, NAF Study

MORNING SUGGESTION:

Matt Emmons lost the Olympic 50 meter rifle event because he aimed his last shot at the wrong goal. What goal will you aim at today? Describe your goal below.

_____

_____

_____

_____

_____

_____

_____

_____

_____

_____

_____

_____

_____

NOON REMINDER:
The goal you described this morning, was it more about passionately pursuing Jesus? Or was it more about being good? Or maybe about avoiding being bad? Or possibly just about surviving?

_____

_____

_____

_____

_____

_____

_____

_____

_____

FINISH THIS SENTENCE:
My goal for the rest of this day is to…

_____

_____

_____

_____

_____

_____

_____

EVENING REFLECTION:

What do you like best about the times when you do passionately pursue Jesus? Try to describe what you enjoy most when you really are about knowing and loving Jesus.

_____

_____

_____

_____

_____

_____

_____

_____

_____

_____

_____

_____

_____

_____

END OF DAY FOCUS:

Go to sleep meditating on what it is like for you when you passionately pursue Jesus.

MORNING QUOTE:
"You blind guides! You strain out a gnat but swallow a camel." (Matthew 23:24)

Straining out gnats is tedious, unrewarding work. If you swallow a gnat, you won't die. You won't even get sick. Gnats may look big and significant when they are floating in your soup, but in reality their presence is relatively inconsequential, especially when you have a camel lodged in your throat.

Ask the Holy Spirit to help you see the gnats at which you tend to strain - things which feel important to you but in actuality make very little difference in how well you know and love Jesus – in each of the areas below.

At church…

With my kids…

In my devotions…

When it comes to food, drink and clothes…

With my friends…

NOON REMINDER:

Have you noticed any gnats this morning, things that feel really important to you but in reality are flea-sized matters in a world of elephant-sized issues? Write about them below.

EVENING REFLECTION:

Take a moment and imagine life without gnats, a life not straining over insignificant things that feel important but really aren't. In a sentence, what would it be like for you?

If you could be gnat free, how would it affect others and how they see you?

_____

_____

_____

_____

_____

_____

How would Jesus like it?

_____

_____

_____

_____

_____

_____

_____

DECISION: From now on, I will treat the following as gnats rather than camels…

_____

_____

_____

_____

END OF DAY FOCUS:
Go to sleep meditating on a gnat-free life.

DAY 5 ___/___/___

MORNING QUOTE:

"Jesus explains the difference between these religious fans and true followers. And the fans are self-righteous and judgmental. They look down on others. But the followers of Jesus are humble and are quick to give the same grace to others that they've received from Jesus Christ." – Kyle, NAF Study

MORNING SUGGESTION:

In each pair, which word best describes you?

humble	self-righteous
ashamed	appreciative
judgmental	understanding
angry	grieved
frustrated	serene
sarcastic	encouraging

Based on your answers, would you say you are living more under:

( ) grace   ( ) law

The cure for pride isn't shame or self-loathing. The cure for pride is the humble act of receiving uncon-ditional love. Sit with your hands open, your palms up, and imagine receiving undeserved, unconditional, unlimited love, forgiveness, grace and favor. Sit and receive the overflow of Heaven, a waterfall of unending grace, more than you can hold. Feel it flood your soul, fill your body like a glass full of cool water, filling you to the top of your head, and overflowing.

After taking time to imagine this love pervading you, go back and mark the pairs above again. What, if anything, changes in your choices?

_____

_____

_____

_____

_____

_____

_____

_____

_____

NOON REMINDER:
Sit before God, but this time with hands clinched and closed. Imagine yourself refusing unconditional love and grace.

Imagine even shaking your fist, and saying to yourself, "I cannot be loved. I must earn everything I get. I will not take favors from anyone."

As you do, feel the reaction in your body.
What are your senses telling you?

_____

_____

_____

_____

_____

_____

_____

_____

_____

_____

_____

_____

_____

If you choose, gradually unclench your fists, open your hands, and ask for unconditional love. It will probably feel like a humbling act, even a child-like act. As you do, sense again the difference, what you are like, what life is like when you freely receive the unconditional love of Jesus.

EVENING REFLECTION:

Again sit with your hands open. Finish these sentences in your mind. Journal your thoughts.

"I can't receive unconditional love because…"

_____

_____

_____

_____

_____

"I must receive unconditional love because…."

_____

_____

_____

_____

_____

"What do you want to put in my hands?"

_____

_____

_____

_____

_____

END OF DAY FOCUS:

Try going to sleep with your hands open.

DAY 6 ___/___/___

MORNING QUOTE:
*"I walked away from God because I thought
He was like you!"* – Eric, NAF Study

MORNING SUGGESTION:
Answer the following questions.

If people thought Jesus was like you,
what would they like about Jesus?

_____

_____

_____

_____

_____

_____

What wouldn't they like?

_____

_____

_____

_____

_____

_____

Would they want to follow Jesus? Why or why not?

_____

_____

_____

_____

NOON REMINDER:
What quality of Jesus do you most adore,
most appreciate? _____

However you answered, open your hands again
and imagine receiving this quality. Imagine it flowing
throughout your body, possessing plenty of it for
yourself and so much it overflows to others.

Try to hold this image in mind during your afternoon.

EVENING REFLECTION:
What difference, if any, did holding the image
of your favorite quality of Jesus filling you have
on your afternoon?

_____

_____

_____

_____

_____

Imagine Jesus standing before you in all His glory. See His holiness in his radiating robes, His compassion in His warm eyes, and His strength in His firm jaw. Then imagine Him stepping into your skin, melding with you, the two of you becoming one.

What is this experience like?

_____

_____

_____

_____

_____

_____

_____

_____

END OF DAY FOCUS:
"Father, I have made you known to them, and will continue to make you known in order that the love you have for me may be in them and that I myself may be in them." (John 17:26)

As you go to sleep, imagine Jesus pulsating within you, His very being inside you, all that He is living in you. Hold this perspective in mind until you drift into slumber.

MORNING QUOTE:
"Come after" = a passionate pursuit

MORNING SUGGESTION:
Journal about what would lead you not just to pursue Jesus, but to pursue Him passionately. What would cause you and move you to deeply desire to know Jesus, to move from rules to relationship?

NOON REMINDER:
List five things you love most, whether it is ice cream, sunsets, flying, children, baseball, whatever!

- _____
- _____
- _____
- _____
- _____

When an artist or inventor creates something, he puts some of himself into his creation. The creation reflects some aspect of the originator. Notice how Jesus is reflected in each of the things you listed.

For example, if you listed "children," in them you can see the playfulness and innocence of the One who created them. Or if you listed "the ocean," then you can sense the unfathomable depths, the great expanse, and the ever-changing-yet-always-the-sameness of the oceans' Creator.

- _____
- _____
- _____
- _____
- _____

How does this exercise affect your passion for Jesus?

_____
_____
_____
_____
_____
_____
_____
_____
_____

EVENING REFLECTION:
"We raised her in Church, but we didn't raise her in Christ." – Distraught father to Kyle, NAF Study

Maybe you were raised in church but not in Christ. Now the choice is yours. How will you live your life, simply in church, going through the motions? Or in Christ, passionately pursuing Him? Describe your thoughts below.

_____

_____

_____

_____

_____

_____

_____

END OF DAY FOCUS:
Can you honestly say to Jesus as you prepare for sleep, "I love you. Above all, I love you and want to know you." If not, again think of your favorite things. See each of your favorite things flowing out of the playfulness, precision, fertility, profundity, power, wisdom and joy of Jesus Himself.

See how He is truly the King of Glory, and love Him.

week six: **decision time!**

WEEK 6: DECISION TIME:

What stood out to you from Lesson 6?

_____
_____
_____
_____
_____
_____
_____
_____
_____
_____
_____
_____

DAY 1   __/__/__

MORNING QUOTE:

"I wish I could come over to your house and knock on your door. Hopefully, I could talk you into letting me come in and sit down for a few minutes. And I would want to sit across the kitchen table from you and look you in the eye and ask you this question…

Have you decided to follow Jesus?" – Kyle, NAF Study

MORNING SUGGESTION:

Rather than Kyle knocking on your door, imagine answering the bell, and it is Jesus Himself. He asks to come in. You offer him coffee or tea. He accepts. You sit down together, and He looks you in the eye, and asks in a voice full of compassion as well as authority: "Have you decided to follow me?"

Journal your response below.

_____

_____

_____

_____

_____

_____

_____

_____

_____

_____

_____

_____

_____

_____

_____

_____

NOON REMINDER:

Why do we have a "noon Reminder" in this journal? Because our decision to follow is not just daily; it is hourly; it is over and over and over.

Ask yourself, "Can I accept the fact that my decision to follow Jesus must be made time and time again, and for the rest of my life?" Write your thoughts below.

_____

_____

_____

_____

_____

_____

_____

_____

_____

_____

_____

_____

_____

_____

_____

_____

_____

_____

_____

EVENING REFLECTION:

Remember the opening challenge of the series described in three letters: "DTR"? The initials stand for Define the Relationship. Maybe the question is now, "How have you redefined the relationship over the last several weeks?" Try to describe your redefined relationship with Jesus as it now stands using the questions below.

How do you define the relationship now?

_____

_____

_____

_____

_____

_____

_____

What is good about it?

_____

_____

_____

_____

_____

_____

_____

What still needs work?

_____

_____

_____

_____

_____

_____

How would Jesus define your relationship?

_____

_____

_____

_____

_____

_____

END OF DAY FOCUS:
A relationship is not like a rock - never changing,
always the same. A relationship is more like a stream,
always flowing, never quite identical moment to
moment, either deepening or growing more shallow,
widening or narrowing, if only little by little.

As you enter sleep, imagine your relationship with
Jesus widening and deepening, and always changing
for the rest of your life and into eternity.

DAY 2 ___/___/___

MORNING QUOTE:

"I was traveling down the I-75, fully convinced that I'm on the I-71, because the roads feel very much the same. Now in hindsight, I should have seen some signs. I'm sure there were some very clear markers that I was on the wrong road. But, I was so sure of myself, I never allowed for the possibility that I was going in the wrong direction."   – Kyle, NAF Study

MORNING SUGGESTION:

Does your mind even allow for the possibility that you might not be a follower of Jesus?

_____

_____

_____

_____

I can't face the idea that I might not be a fully devoted follower of Jesus because...

_____

_____

_____

_____

I am fully willing to consider the fact that I might not be a true follower of Jesus because…

_____

_____

_____

_____

_____

_____

NOON REMINDER:

"Enter through the narrow gate. For wide is the gate and broad is the road that leads to destruction, and many enter through it. But small is the gate and narrow the road that leads to life, and only a few find it." (Matthew 7:13-14)

Read the passage three times. Underline the phrase that stands out to you most. Write why this phrase stands out.

_____

_____

_____

_____

_____

_____

EVENING REFLECTION:

Kyle missed the signs that he was on I-75 rather than I-71. What are each of these "signs" below saying about you, and whether or not you are a follower of Jesus?

Your conscience.

_____

_____

_____

Your friends.

_____

_____

_____

Your family.

_____

_____

_____

Your mentor.

_____

_____

_____

Your lifestyle.

_____

_____

_____

Holy Spirit.

_____

_____

_____

END OF DAY FOCUS:
"I'm just asking: what if many of us are traveling down what we think is the narrow road that leads to life, but we're actually on the broad road that leads to destruction? What if we have hit the cruise control and are traveling through life singing along to Christian Radio with a Jesus fish on the bumper, completely unaware that we are headed to destruction? I'm not trying to make you paranoid or fearful. I believe that nothing can separate us from the love of God and my confidence is in Him who can keep me from falling. But clearly the Bible teaches that there are those who have a false assurance of salvation.

So, what if one day Jesus returns, and all kinds of good church-going folks find out that, in the end, they were never on the right road? I'm just asking, is it possible that you think you're a follower, but you're really just a fan? I don't want to make people unnecessarily question where they will spend eternity, but how can you read Matthew 7:13-14 without raising the question?"

As you read the above paragraph,
was your heart at peace or troubled?

MORNING QUOTE:
"Not everyone who says to me, 'Lord, Lord,' will enter the Kingdom of Heaven, but only he who does the will of my Father who is in heaven. Many will say to me on that day, 'Lord, Lord, did we not prophesy in your name, and in your name drive out demons and perform many miracles?' Then I will tell them plainly, 'I never knew you. Away from me, you evildoers!'"
(Matthew 7:21-23)

"Jesus doesn't say this will happen to a few. He doesn't say some. He says many."   – Kyle, NAF Study

Kyle asks two big questions in the episode.
Try to answer for yourself.

Have I determined that I am a follower because I say I am a follower rather than because I act like a follower?

_____

_____

_____

_____

_____

_____

Have I determined that I am a follower based on religious measurements rather than loving deeds?

_____

_____

_____

_____

NOON REMINDER:

I believe I am a follower of Jesus because…

_____

_____

_____

_____

EVENING REFLECTION:

Today could you be called an "evildoer"?
Why or why not?

_____

_____

_____

_____

END OF DAY FOCUS:

Has answering today's tough questions drawn you closer to Jesus or led you further away? Use today's final moments trying to discern why.

MORNING QUOTE:
Eric: *"You don't need to be here. Go home."*
Natalie: *"Why? Just because I don't know her name?"*
Eric: *"Because you don't want to."*

MORNING SUGGESTION:
Whose names don't you want to know? Think of the people in your life. Which person's name don't you care about? Make a list, even if it must be by description in the cases where you really don't know the person's name.

_____

_____

_____

_____

_____

What similarities do you see in these people that would lead them to be people whose names you don't want to know?

_____

_____

_____

_____

NOON REMINDER:

Whose names have you wanted, and not wanted to know, in your interactions so far today? Make two lists, then describe why.

Wanted	Not Wanted

EVENING REFLECTION:

Are you a follower of Jesus based on this paragraph?

"One of the clues you may be more fan than follower is that when I asked 'Are you a follower' your mind immediately went to the fact that you come to church, put some money in the plate, volunteer from time to time. Let me just ask you a really blunt question: do you think God needs your help?

"Do you think you're earning His gratitude by ticking off a list of religious busywork? No, I'm not saying that attending church or giving money or reading your Bible are bad things to do. But think for a second. Why would those things matter to God? I believe they only matter to God as an expression of your closeness to Him. He doesn't need your help, you aren't going to impress Him, but He does long for you to be close to Him, for you to know Him intimately. And really, that's the question, isn't it? Do you know Jesus? Does He know you? That's what it comes down to. Does He have your heart? Is He your everything? Do you invest more in your relationship with Him than any other relationship? I think we sometimes confuse knowing about Jesus with knowing Jesus. But there is a difference between knowledge and intimacy."
– Kyle, NAF Study

END OF DAY FOCUS:
Ask Jesus what matters to Him as you complete your day.

DAY 5 ___/___/___

MORNING QUOTE:

Natalie: *"This is what we're supposed to do. Right? I mean. We decide that we want to follow Jesus. We sell all our stuff. We quit our good jobs. We sell our homes. I mean, it stinks, but we suck it up and do it anyway, right? I mean, this is what we're supposed to do, isn't it?"*
Eric: *"It's what I'm supposed to do."*
Natalie: *"I don't want people to say I'm fake."*
Eric: *"Nat...It's not how much we give. It's not how much we do. You know what separates the real from the fakes? Love."*

MORNING REFLECTION:
Think about this question carefully:
When do you love others the best?

_____ When I focus on trying to manufacture unconditional love for others.

_____ When I focus on receiving the unconditional love of Jesus for me.

What do you learn from your answer?

_____

_____

_____

_____

NOON REMINDER:
To follow Jesus is to love. Imagine Jesus encountering those you will likely encounter today. Envision how he would look at them, what he would see, how he would act toward them.

_____

_____

_____

_____

_____

EVENING REFLECTION:
Would you say you have been a poser today or the real deal? Journal your response.

_____

_____

_____

_____

_____

END OF DAY FOCUS:

Consider the question: Is Jesus a poser? Does he just pretend to love people or does He really love them? What does your answer mean to you?

_____

_____

_____

_____

_____

_____

_____

_____

_____

_____

_____

_____

_____

_____

_____

_____

_____

_____

_____

MORNING QUOTE:

"Jesus is not impressed because your name is on your bumper sticker, or because you have Christian music on your ipod, or because you never miss a weekend at church, or you give to all the right causes. And those things are all good, but they are only good to the extent that they are done out of love for Him. Jesus says that He wants us to love Him with all of our heart and soul and mind and strength. And then He says, 'Love your neighbor as yourself.' It is love that reveals us to be real followers of Jesus Christ...Jesus wants you to love Him enough to take up your cross. So for you, which is it? What road have you chosen? Fan, or Follower? It all comes down to love."
– Kyle, NAF Study

Imagine yourself putting love at the top of your to-do list today. Imagine yourself encouraging the various people you will likely see, and overflowing with love, concern, care. Jot some notes on what it would be like, how it would be different from other days.

_____

_____

_____

_____

NOON REMINDER:
Who is the best lover you have encountered?
Your grandmother? Your spouse? A college friend?
Describe that person below.

_____

_____

_____

_____

_____

_____

EVENING REFLECTION:
Imagine someone you know answering the question
from today's noon reminder with your name. What
would you want them to write? How would you like
another to describe you?

_____

_____

_____

_____

_____

_____

END OF DAY FOCUS:
Close your day praying prayers of love for
those you care about.

MORNING QUOTE:

"'Lord, please help me. Because I know that without You, I can do nothing. And I know that without love I am nothing. Without love, it doesn't matter what I say. It doesn't matter how much faith I have. It doesn't matter how much I give. The only way I can be anything is if I am Yours and the only way people will know that I am Yours is if I love. That was my father. It still is."
– Natalie reading from her dad's journal, NAF Study

Imagine someone finding and reading this journal of yours. How would you feel about it?

_____

_____

_____

_____

_____

_____

_____

_____

_____

_____

_____

_____

If your focus was on "self" you might be embarrassed or possibly proud. If your focus was on Jesus, how would you feel?

_____

_____

_____

_____

_____

_____

_____

_____

NOON REMINDER:
Who comes to mind from your study group?
Write a prayer for him or her.

_____

_____

_____

_____

_____

_____

_____

_____

_____

EVENING REFLECTION:

What kinds of things do you wish you had written in this journal?

_____
_____
_____
_____
_____
_____
_____
_____
_____
_____
_____
_____
_____
_____
_____
_____
_____
_____
_____
_____
_____
_____

This is your last entry in the Not a Fan Follower's Journal. What practices do you see yourself including in your life in order to best continue to build your relationship with Jesus as His follower?

_____

_____

_____

_____

_____

_____

_____

_____

_____

_____

_____

_____

_____

_____

_____

_____

_____

_____

_____

_____

_____

_____

_____

END OF DAY FOCUS:
Try softly singing or humming these words as you enter sleep:

I have decided to follow Jesus.

I have decided to follow Jesus.

I have decided to follow Jesus.

No turning back, no turning back.

following.

LUKE
9:23

FOLLOWING.

Congratulations on completing your journal. We hope that this personal journey will only be the beginning of your daily commitment to follow Jesus.

So now that you have decided to follow Jesus, what's next? If you really want to follow Jesus then you must let Him lead. Consider starting on your knees and praying for His guidance.

*"If anyone
would come after me,
he must deny himself
and take up his cross daily
and follow me."*

(Luke 9:23)

Not a fan is more than just a small group study. It is a Movement. Join the thousands of others around the world that have declared "I am not a fan."

www.notafan.com
(the site)

www.facebook.com/notafan
(the movement)

www.twitter.com/iamnotafan
(the talk)

www.youtube.com/notafantv
(the videos)

Notes:

Notes: